ROYAL COURT

Royal Court Theatre presents

NOTES ON FALLING LEAVES

by Ayub Khan-Din

First performance at the Royal Court Jerwood Theatre Downstairs
Sloane Square, London on 11 February 2004.

Supported by

JERWOOD
NEW PLAYWRIGHTS

with additional support from
THE ROYAL COLLEGE OF PSYCHIATRISTS

NOTES ON FALLING LEAVES

by **Ayub Khan-Din**

Cast in order of appearance
Woman **Pam Ferris**
Man **Ralf Little**

Director **Marianne Elliott**
Lighting Designer **Trevor Wallace**
Sound Designer **Ian Dickinson**
Casting **Lisa Makin**
Production Manager **Paul Handley**
Company Voice Work **Patsy Rodenburg**
Costume Designer/Supervisor **Iona Kenrick**

THE COMPANY

Ayub Khan-Din (writer)
For the Royal Court: East is East (co-production
Tamasha/Birmingham Rep; also Manhattan Theatre
Club, New York/Oldham Coliseum/ Theatre
Royal/Stratford East/New Vic Theatre Stoke)
Other theatre includes: Last Dance at Dum Dum
(New Ambassadors).
Film includes: East is East (Assassin Films/BBC).
Screenplays include: Belmondo JI (Raboon
Pictures/FilmFour), Slow Down Arthur, Stick To
Thirty (DNA Films/Raboon Pictures), The
Competition (Working Title Films/Raboon Pictures).
Awards include: 1997 Writers' Guild Award for Best
West End Play and Best New Writer, and the John
Whiting Award for East is East; 1999 Audience
Award for Best First Film, Evening Standard Award
for Best Film, Alexander Korda Award for
Outstanding British Film of the Year, the British
Independent Film Award for Best Original
Screenplay, and the Critics' Circle Award for Best
Screenplay for East is East; and British Asian Award
for Film and Television.

Ian Dickinson (sound designer)
For the Royal Court: Loyal Women, The Sugar
Syndrome, Blood, Playing the Victim, Fallout, Flesh
Wound, Hitchcock Blonde (& Lyric), Black Milk,
Crazyblackmuthafuckin'self, Caryl Churchill Shorts,
Imprint, Mother Teresa is Dead, Push Up, Workers
Writes, Fucking Games, Herons, Cutting Through
the Carnival.
Other theatre includes: Port (Royal Exchange,
Manchester); Night of the Soul (RSC Barbican);
Eyes of the Kappa (Gate); Crime and Punishment in
Dalston (Arcola Theatre); Search and Destroy
(New End, Hampstead); Phaedra, Three Sisters,
The Shaughraun, Writer's Cramp (Royal Lyceum,
Edinburgh); The Whore's Dream (RSC Fringe,
Edinburgh); As You Like It, An Experienced Woman
Gives Advice, Present Laughter, The Philadelphia
Story, Wolks World, Poor Superman, Martin
Yesterday, Fast Food, Coyote Ugly, Prizenight
(Royal Exchange, Manchester).
Ian is Head of Sound at the Royal Court.

Marianne Elliott (director)
For the Royal Court: The Sugar Syndrome,
Local.
Previously she was an Artistic Director of the
Royal Exchange Theatre, Manchester where
her directing credits include: Port, Design for
Living, Les Blancs, As You Like It, A Woman of
No Importance, Nude with Violin, Fast Food,
Martin Yesterday, Deep Blue Sea, Mad for It,
Poor Superman, I Have Been Here Before.
Other theatre includes: The Little Foxes
(Donmar); Terracotta (Hampstead/
Birmingham Rep).
The Associate Director post is supported by
the BBC through the Gerald Chapman Fund.
Marianne is an Associate Director at the
Royal Court.

Pam Ferris
For the Royal Court: Devil's Gateway, Lucky
Chance, The Grace of Mary Traverse, Apples;
The Queen and I, Road (co-production with
Out of Joint/tour).
Other theatre includes: The Importance of
Being Earnest (New Zealand); Hamlet, The
Merchant of Venice, Othello (Monthly
Repertory Theatre, New Zealand); Arabian
Nights, Bleak House, Science Fictions,
Cymbeline, La Ronde (Shared Experience),
Romeo and Juliet; The Caucasian Chalk Circle,
The Country Wife (Sheffield Theatre);
The Cherry Orchard (Oxford Playhouse);
Cat on a Hot Tin Roof, Bluebird of
Unhappiness, Ridley Walker (Royal Exchange,
Manchester); The Seagull (Oxford Theatre
and tour); The Vagina Monologues (Old Vic
Productions/New Ambassador's); Roots,
Closing Time (RNT and tour).
Television includes: The Bill, Casualty, Oranges
are not the Only Fruit, Darling Buds of May,
Roots, Middlemarch, Death of a Salesman,
The Tenant of Wildfell Hall, Where the Heart
Is, Our Mutual Friend, The Turn of The Screw,
First Sign of Madness, Nicholas Nickleby,
Sweet Revenge, Linda Green, Pollyanna,
Paradise Heights, Family, Clocking Off,
Rosemary and Thyme, French and Saunders
Xmas Special 2003.
Film includes: Matilda, Death to Smoochy,
Harry Potter and the Prisoner of Azkaban,
Piccadilly Jim, Meantime.
Radio includes: Class of '81.
Awards include: Actress of the Year 2003,
Michael Elliott Trust Award.

Ralf Little

For the Royal Court: Presence (Olivier nomination 2002 for Most Promising Performer). Other theatre includes: Love on the Dole (RNT). Television includes: Two Pints of Lager & A Packet of Crisps (4 series), The Eustace Bros., Pear Shaped – North Face of the Eiger, Up Late with Ralf Little, Paradise Heights, The Bill, Aladdin, The Royle Family (3 series), Always & Everyone, Flint Street Nativity, Bostock's Cup, The Ward, Heartbeat, Sloggers (2 series). Film includes: Zemanovaload, Frozen, Fat Slags, Poison Arrows, 24 Hour Party People, Al's Lads, Harry on the Boat.

Trevor Wallace (lighting designer)

For the Royal Court: Rampage, A Day in Dull Armour, Graffitti.
Other theatre includes: Golden Boy, Nobody's Perfect, The Book of the Banshee, Kit and the Widow – The Fat Lady Sings (Yvonne Arnaud Theatre, Guildford); Cabaret, Sweet Charity (Electric Theatre, Guildford); The Changeling (Sandpit Theatre, St Albans); Comedy of Errors, Grimm Tales, Richard III, Cyrano de Bergerac, Les Enfants du Paradis (Minack Theatre, Cornwall).
Trevor is the Deputy Head of Lighting at the Royal Court.

ROYAL COURT
JERWOOD THEATRE DOWNSTAIRS

25 February – 6 March
Massive Company's production of
THE SONS OF CHARLIE PAORA
by **Lennie James**
Directed by Sam Scott

Charlie Paora is dead and buried. One night in a garage in Mangere, South Auckland, a group of young men gather to acknowledge the passing of their mentor, father figure and rugby coach Charlie Paora. The tension heightens when the real son and daughter of Charlie Paora turn up. This is a story of love, loyalty, life and death.

Cast includes
Wesley Dowdell, Joe Folau, Kiri Lightfoot, Max Palamo, Liston Rua, Foma'i Taito and Jason Webb.
Set & costumes
Tracey Collins
Lighting Bryan Caldwell

BOX OFFICE
020 7565 5000
www.royalcourttheatre.com

THE ENGLISH STAGE COMPANY
AT THE ROYAL COURT

The English Stage Company at the Royal Court opened in 1956 as a subsidised theatre producing new British plays, international plays and some classical revivals.

The first artistic director George Devine aimed to create a writers' theatre, 'a place where the dramatist is acknowledged as the fundamental creative force in the theatre and where the play is more important than the actors, the director, the designer'. The urgent need was to find a contemporary style in which the play, the acting, direction and design are all combined. He believed that 'the battle will be a long one to continue to create the right conditions for writers to work in'.

Devine aimed to discover 'hard-hitting, uncompromising writers whose plays are stimulating, provocative and exciting'. The Royal Court production of John Osborne's Look Back in Anger in May 1956 is now seen as the decisive starting point of modern British drama and the policy created a new generation of British playwrights. The first wave included John Osborne, Arnold Wesker, John Arden, Ann Jellicoe, N F Simpson and Edward Bond. Early seasons included new international plays by Bertolt Brecht, Eugène Ionesco, Samuel Beckett, Jean-Paul Sartre and Marguerite Duras.

The theatre started with the 400-seat proscenium arch Theatre Downstairs, and then in 1969 opened a second theatre, the 60-seat studio Theatre Upstairs. Some productions transfer to the West End, such as Terry Johnson's Hitchcock Blonde, Caryl Churchill's Far Away, Conor McPherson's The Weir, Kevin Elyot's Mouth to Mouth and My Night With Reg. The Royal Court also co-produces plays which have transferred to the West End or toured internationally, such as Sebastian Barry's The Steward of Christendom and Mark Ravenhill's Shopping and Fucking (with Out of Joint), Martin McDonagh's The Beauty Queen Of Leenane (with Druid Theatre Company), Ayub Khan-Din's East is East (with Tamasha Theatre Company, and now a feature film).

Since 1994 the Royal Court's artistic policy has again been vigorously directed to finding and producing a new generation of playwrights. The writers include Joe Penhall, Rebecca Prichard, Michael Wynne, Nick Grosso, Judy Upton, Meredith Oakes, Sarah Kane, Anthony Neilson, Judith Johnson, James Stock, Jez Butterworth, Marina Carr, Phyllis Nagy, Simon Bluck, Martin McDonagh, Mark Ravenhill, Ayub Khan-Din, Tamantha Hammerschlag, Jess Walters, Ché Walker, Conor McPherson, Simon

photo: Andy Chopping

Stephens, Richard Bean, Roy Williams, Gary Mitchell, Mick Mahoney, Rebecca Gilman, Christopher Shinn, Kia Corthron, David Gieselmann, Marius von Mayenburg, David Eldridge, Leo Butler, Zinnie Harris, Grae Cleugh, Roland Schimmelpfennig, DeObia Oparei, Vassily Sigarev, the Presnyakov Brothers and Lucy Prebble. This expanded programme of new plays has been made possible through the support of A.S.K Theater Projects and the Skirball Foundation, the Jerwood Charitable Foundation the American Friends of the Royal Court Theatre and many in association with the Royal National Theatre Studio.

In recent years there have been record-breaking productions at the box office, with capacity houses for Roy Williams' Fallout, Terry Johnson's Hitchcock Blonde, Caryl Churchill's A Number, Jez Butterworth's The Night Heron, Rebecca Gilman's Boy Gets Girl, Kevin Elyot's Mouth to Mouth, David Hare's My Zinc Bed and Conor McPherson's The Weir, which transferred to the West End in October 1998 and ran for nearly two years at the Duke of York's Theatre.

The newly refurbished theatre in Sloane Square opened in February 2000, with a policy still inspired by the first artistic director George Devine. The Royal Court is an international theatre for new plays and new playwrights, and the work shapes contemporary drama in Britain and overseas.

AWARDS FOR
THE ROYAL COURT

Jez Butterworth won the 1995 George Devine Award, the Writers' Guild New Writer of the Year Award, the Evening Standard Award for Most Promising Playwright and the Olivier Award for Best Comedy for Mojo.

The Royal Court was the overall winner of the 1995 Prudential Award for the Arts for creativity, excellence, innovation and accessibility. The Royal Court Theatre Upstairs won the 1995 Peter Brook Empty Space Award for innovation and excellence in theatre.

Michael Wynne won the 1996 Meyer-Whitworth Award for The Knocky. Martin McDonagh won the 1996 George Devine Award, the 1996 Writers' Guild Best Fringe Play Award, the 1996 Critics' Circle Award and the 1996 Evening Standard Award for Most Promising Playwright for The Beauty Queen of Leenane. Marina Carr won the 19th Susan Smith Blackburn Prize (1996/7) for Portia Coughlan. Conor McPherson won the 1997 George Devine Award, the 1997 Critics' Circle Award and the 1997 Evening Standard Award for Most Promising Playwright for The Weir. Ayub Khan-Din won the 1997 Writers' Guild Awards for Best West End Play and Writers' Guild New Writer of the Year and the 1996 John Whiting Award for East is East (co-production with Tamasha).

At the 1998 Tony Awards, Martin McDonagh's The Beauty Queen of Leenane (co-production with Druid Theatre Company) won four awards including Garry Hynes for Best Director and was nominated for a further two. Eugene Ionesco's The Chairs (co-production with Theatre de Complicite) was nominated for six Tony awards. David Hare won the 1998 Time Out Live Award for Outstanding Achievement and six awards in New York including the Drama League, Drama Desk and New York Critics Circle Award for Via Dolorosa. Sarah Kane won the 1998 Arts Foundation Fellowship in Playwriting. Rebecca Prichard won the 1998 Critics' Circle Award for Most Promising Playwright for Yard Gal (co-production with Clean Break).

Conor McPherson won the 1999 Olivier Award for Best New Play for The Weir. The Royal Court won the 1999 ITI Award for Excellence in International Theatre. Sarah Kane's Cleansed was judged Best Foreign Language Play in 1999 by Theater Heute in Germany. Gary Mitchell won the 1999 Pearson Best Play Award for Trust. Rebecca Gilman was joint winner of the 1999 George Devine Award and won the 1999 Evening Standard Award for Most Promising Playwright for The Glory of Living.

In 1999, the Royal Court won the European theatre prize New Theatrical Realities, presented at Taormina Arte in Sicily, for its efforts in recent years in discovering and producing the work of young British dramatists.

Roy Williams and Gary Mitchell were joint winners of the George Devine Award 2000 for Most Promising Playwright for Lift Off and The Force of Change respectively. At the Barclays Theatre Awards 2000 presented by the TMA, Richard Wilson won the Best Director Award for David Gieselmann's Mr Kolpert and Jeremy Herbert won the Best Designer Award for Sarah Kane's 4.48 Psychosis. Gary Mitchell won the Evening Standard's Charles Wintour Award 2000 for Most Promising Playwright for The Force of Change. Stephen Jeffreys' I Just Stopped by to See The Man won an AT&T: On Stage Award 2000.

David Eldridge's Under the Blue Sky won the Time Out Live Award 2001 for Best New Play in the West End. Leo Butler won the George Devine Award 2001 for Most Promising Playwright for Redundant. Roy Williams won the Evening Standard's Charles Wintour Award 2001 for Most Promising Playwright for Clubland. Grae Cleugh won the 2001 Olivier Award for Most Promising Playwright for Fucking Games. Richard Bean was joint winner of the George Devine Award 2002 for Most Promising Playwright for Under the Whaleback. Caryl Churchill won the 2002 Evening Standard Award for Best New Play for A Number. Vassily Sigarev won the 2002 Evening Standard Charles Wintour Award for Most Promising Playwright for Plasticine. Ian MacNeil won the 2002 Evening Standard Award for Best Design for A Number and Plasticine. Peter Gill won the 2002 Critics' Circle Award for Best New Play for The York Realist (English Touring Theatre). Ché Walker won the 2003 George Devine Award for Most Promising Playwright for Flesh Wound.

ROYAL COURT BOOKSHOP

The bookshop offers a wide range of playtexts and theatre books, with over 1,000 titles. Located in the downstairs Bar and Food area, the bookshop is open Monday to Saturday, afternoons and evenings.

Many Royal Court playtexts are available for just £2 including works by Harold Pinter, Caryl Churchill, Rebecca Gilman, Martin Crimp, Sarah Kane, Conor McPherson, Ayub Khan-Din, Timberlake Wertenbaker and Roy Williams.

For information on titles and special events, Email: bookshop@royalcourttheatre.com
Tel: 020 7565 5024

PROGRAMME SUPPORTERS

The Royal Court (English Stage Company Ltd) receives its principal funding from London Arts. It is also supported financially by a wide range of private companies and public bodies and earns the remainder of its income from the box office and its own trading activities.
The Royal Borough of Kensington & Chelsea gives an annual grant to the Royal Court Young Writers' Programme.

The Jerwood Charitable Foundation continues to support new plays by new playwrights through the Jerwood New Playwrights series. Since 1993 A.S.K. Theater Projects and the Skirball Foundation have funded a Playwrights' Programme at the theatre. Bloomberg Mondays, the Royal Court's reduced price ticket scheme, is supported by Bloomberg. Over the past seven years the BBC has supported the Gerald Chapman Fund for directors.

ROYAL COURT
SLOANE SQUARE

**INTERNATIONAL
PLAYWRIGHTS SEASON 2004**
A Genesis Project

5 – 28 February
ALMOST
NOTHING and
AT THE TABLE
by **Marcos Barbosa**
translated by Mark O'Thomas
Two new plays from Brazil

Director Roxana Silbert
Designer Anthony MacIlwaine
Lighting Chahine Yavroyan
Sound Matt McKenzie

Cast Mark Bonnar, Lorna Gayle,
Mido Hamada, Karl Johnson, Nina
Sosanya, Ewan Stewart, Jonathan
Timmins and Robert Timmins.

5 – 27 March
LADYBIRD
by **Vassily Sigarev**
translated by Sasha Dugdale
Director Ramin Gray
Designer Lizzie Clachan
Lighting Nigel Edwards
Sound Ian Dickinson

30 March – 3 April
CUBAN
READINGS

**Visit the website for details of
additional events**

BOX OFFICE
020 7565 5000
www.royalcourttheatre.com

London Government

ARTS COUNCIL
ENGLAND

FOR THE ROYAL COURT

JERWOOD
NEW PLAYWRIGHTS

Since 1993 Jerwood New Playwrights have contributed to some of the Royal Court's most successful productions, including SHOPPING AND FUCKING by Mark Ravenhill (co-production with Out of Joint), EAST IS EAST by Ayub Khan-Din (co-production with Tamasha), THE BEAUTY QUEEN OF LEENANE by Martin McDonagh (co-production with Druid Theatre Company), THE WEIR by Conor McPherson, REAL CLASSY AFFAIR by Nick Grosso, THE FORCE OF CHANGE by Gary Mitchell, ON RAFTERY'S HILL by Marina Carr (co-production with Druid Theatre Company), 4.48 PSYCHOSIS by Sarah Kane, UNDER THE BLUE SKY by David Eldridge, PRESENCE by David Harrower, HERONS by Simon Stephens, CLUBLAND by Roy Williams, REDUNDANT by Leo Butler, NIGHTINGALE AND CHASE by Zinnie Harris, FUCKING GAMES by Grae Cleugh, BEDBOUND by Enda Walsh, THE PEOPLE ARE FRIENDLY by Michael Wynne, OUTLYING ISLANDS by David Greig and IRON by Rona Munro, UNDER THE WHALEBACK by Richard Bean, FLESH WOUND by Ché Walker, FALLOUT by Roy Williams and FOOD CHAIN by Mick Mahoney. This season Jerwood New Playwrights are supporting NOTES ON FALLING LEAVES by Ayub Khan-Din.

The Jerwood Charitable Foundation is a registered charity dedicated to imaginative and responsible funding and sponsorship of the arts, education, design and other areas of human endeavour and excellence.

HERONS by Simon Stephens
(photo: Pete Jones)

EAST IS EAST by Ayub Khan-Din
(photo: Robert Day)

NOTES ON FALLING LEAVES

Ayub Khan-Din

for

Zaffa

'ere y'are now

Characters

MAN, *twenty-six*

WOMAN, *early fifties*

Leaves completely cover the stage and wings. A rusty iron bench is centre stage. A WOMAN *in her early fifties stands upstage centre in the semi-darkness. We hear the sound of a film projector start.*

The WOMAN *has short grey hair. She wears a large maternity-type dress with a Peter Pan collar. She plucks at the waist of the dress all the time, as if irritated in some way. On her arm she carries a handbag. When she moves, it is in a stooped shuffle. She slowly bends and picks up a leaf and whispers to it and then drops it again. She shuffles towards the bench and contemplates it. She knows there is something she has to do with it, but it doesn't come to her.*

Beat.

She looks about her, a pained expression on her face. She moans little moans. She comes to the front of the bench and lowers herself down towards the seat, but misses it completely. Slowly she squats down in front of it, whispering to the leaves as she picks them up. Upstage a MAN, *twenty-six, slowly follows her forward. He lights a cigarette. He clears his throat. He does this throughout his speech. He stands and stares at her. In his hand, he holds a bright pink child's drinking beaker with a lid and two handles.*

MAN. I stayed at the house last night. Your house . . . Last night . . .

He clears his throat again. The WOMAN *does not acknowledge him but carries on handling the leaves.*

I stayed in your house last night . . . Our house. The house we all lived in.

The WOMAN *pays no attention to anything the* MAN *says. Her focus is never on him.*

WOMAN. Hanawahd. I couldevin . . .

She moans. He clears his throat again.

MAN. It was there . . . but it wasn't . . . bit like you really. Shadowed. Dirt on the handle of the fridge. Fingerprints that belong to fingers that don't feel any more. I touched them. Ran my fingers over them. You. Everything I touched had you on them. Every room had conversations in them.

It was all there exactly as I remembered it, nothing changed. But it's a dead house. If houses can die, then your house is dead. The girl I'd brought with me thought it was spooky. She sat in a chair afraid and wouldn't move. Followed me about like you did . . . Could hardly tell her to 'Fuck off and sit down,' could I? It was cold. Soulless. There was still a distinctive odour of stale piss around the place . . . not your fault, I know. She smelt it. The girl. The moment we walked in. She didn't let on but I know she smelt it. I knew it was coming at the top of road. Even before I put the key in the back door. You'll be pleased to know I used the back door. Even though I'd brought a visitor. It made me laugh . . . Shocking, to come to your boyfriend's parents' house permeated with the smell of age-old piss.

I didn't care. 'What d'you think?' I said in a very 'I've just had the whole place redesigned' kind of voice. 'Oh it's very nice,' she said. 'It's council,' I said. 'Oh right . . . I've never been in one before.' She sat down in your chair. She probably thinks all council houses smell of piss. She lives with her parents in a house in Mayfair . . . It's very nice. You would have liked it. Not a whiff of piss in that place. I watched her. I think I was enjoying her discomfort. She didn't know what to say or do. She didn't seem to want to touch anything . . .

She'd have freaked if I'd told her she was sat in your chair. Your pissy old chair . . . I could still make out the ash in the carpet from your fags missing the ashtray.

I began to resent her being there. She looked clean and fresh. So was I, but I was part of it . . . I still belonged there. Even now, after all this time. It all looked the same. But dead. There was a Christmas tree bulb on the floor behind the telly . . . Papers still in the two pouffes by the electric fire. Bills behind that awful glass swan. Are they called pouffes? You used to call them pouffes. I've heard them called Ottomans . . . Ottoman pouffes? Probably a grain of truth in that. They were partial to taking it up the shitter I believe . . . I fucked her in our kid's old bedroom. She wouldn't use yours or mine. The only two with beds still in them. The others took theirs with them when they left. Four gone, two to go. Mine and yours. Not that I'm gonna take mine . . . I stuck my mattress on the floor in our kid's room. Hope you don't mind . . .

It was dead . . . the sex. Dead sex in a dead house. Cold, clammy, shadowed, dead sex.

Offstage we hear the faint sound of a vacuum cleaner moved across a floor.

Sex with the smell of piss and decay. It was hard getting into her, entering her . . . I hope you don't mind me mentioning this to you . . . it's not therapy or owt . . . I'm not looking for a reaction from you. We're well

beyond that now . . . I just feel I can. 'Cause you don't
hear or understand and it helps me in some odd . . .
fucked-up kind of way. Where was I? It was hard . . .
I think she was a virgin. I don't know . . . I've never
consciously had a virgin, mother, though it's not
through lack of trying. It's not something you ask, is
it? We haven't been seeing each other long. A couple
of weeks. I don't know why I asked her to come.

There was blood . . . lots of it . . . even in the dark I
could see it dark on the sheets. I understand blood . . .
I know there's something wrong when I see blood.
There's something you can do. She didn't scream
out like I've heard virgins are supposed to do their
first time. I'm not saying I was disappointed or
anything . . . A scream I understand . . . pain I understand. She's worried about the blood stains on the
sheets. She wants to wash them. Your sheets. Your
best sheets. The ones you won at Bingo. Your big win.
Remember how happy you were when you won all
those prizes and they sent you home in a black taxi?
Sheets, a glass swan that you could put flowers in, a
photo album for all your happy memories, a thatched
cottage tea set . . .

I told her not to worry about the sheets as everything's
being dumped by the council next week. Your house
and its contents. All our lives. Going to the dump.
It freaked her out even more. She cried. I was worried,
in an oddly detached way, that she might become
hysterical. I ran her a bath, I thought it might help . . .
I sat outside the door listening to the water splash
about. I took a towel in for her . . . she stood up in the
bath, smiling, waiting for me to wrap her up in the
towel and lift her out, the way you used to do to us
when we were kids . . . She looked fuckin' horny
standing there . . . drips of water running down her
body . . . I started to get a hard-on again. But then you

were standing next to her . . . wet and scared with
your saggy old tits dangling down and your sad old
bush . . . Sons shouldn't see their mothers' bush . . .
They shouldn't give directions on how to wash from
outside the bathroom . . . She looked at me strangely
and took the towel.

Sitting in her water, I washed the blood off my cock . . .
all looked a bit like fuckin' *Psycho*. By the time I'd
finished she was asleep. I lay awake and listened for
your snores.

Nothing . . . you're not there. I sit on the stairs and
listen to the house. It's breathing low and shallow . . .
it must be getting harder now . . . can't be long.
I wandered round the rooms in the blackness . . . Just
like you used to do. What were you looking for . . . Who
were you whispering to in the dark? Would I bump
into your ghost . . . but you're not dead . . . you're as
good as, if you don't mind me saying . . . you may as
well be . . . everything's basically working but . . .
I can't speak to your spirit if you're not dead . . . bit
of a disappointment in the dead parent conversation
department. I've a friend who speaks to his dead
mother all the time in his head. He finds this very
comforting . . . I can't. You're not dead . . . Which is
inconvenient sometimes. It feels like you're dead . . .
I try to pretend that you're dead, but you won't die.
You blink. It's amazing how much life there is in a
blink. I think sometimes, you're about to say
something . . . but then you don't. You blink.

I'm here for the others. I'm here 'cause it's expected.
When I'm in London I don't even think about you.
You rarely cross my mind. 'I won't take my coat off,
I'm not stopping,' so to speak.

*He clears his throat again. He hums to himself. He
lights a cigarette.*

Last night. In the middle of the night. I walked our
walk again. That walk. The walk we took that day.
The girl would've freaked if she'd woken and I wasn't
there. But I thought . . . Fuck it! I'm going! Fuck it!
This'll be the last time I'm here. The last time the
house is here.

I leave. It's three o'clock in the morning and I'm
running through the estate to the medical centre. Past
St. Joeys, past what's his name's house who was in my
class at school and got his eye poked out in a fight at
the fifth-year disco . . . Not so fucking hard now are
you, you one eyed bastard! Through the shitty precinct,
six derelict shops, a chippy and a fuckin' Spar.

I'm outside the medical centre. It's a burnt-out shell.
I wander through what's left. I'm in the room. That
room. It smells of piss as well. Used needles on the
floor . . . It's dark in here . . . empty. No sun. When we
were here, there was bright, bright sunshine, streaming
through the windows. A doctor and six fuckin' medical
students!

Six fuckin' students and . . .

'I'm afraid she'll have to have more tests.'

Six fuckin' students and . . .

'It won't get any better.'

Six fuckin' students and everything that was, before
we came into this room, has gone! You're brought
back in and you sit next to me. You smile politely.
That working-class deference to authority . . . I can't
hear anything. I can't see anything. I'm not sure if I'm
still breathing. There's something in my stomach. It's
starting to rise into my chest. It's in my throat.

I'm out the door. We're walking back together. You
and me. Mother and son . . . I want to . . . I want . . .

There's something in my throat. I force it down.
You're by my side. You look worried. I've never seen
that look before. You look scared. I shouldn't be
seeing this. Children don't see these things. They
can't. They just can't. I walk faster. You're trying to
keep up. Pathetic little steps . . . Looking up at me . . .

'What did he say?'

I force it down.

'Must be the change.'

I force it down.

Not here. I've got to get home. I walk faster and faster.
The sun's shining, it's a beautiful day. People sit on
their steps talking, drinking tea. Through the precinct,
busy shops, people queue in the chippy. 'Do we need
owt from t' Spar?' I force it down. It aches . . . I'm
beginning to ache . . . Oh, Mam, it hurts . . . it hurts so
bad . . . I want to scream. I'm screaming inside! And
you run to keep up. Cubs and Brownies playing games
outside St. Joeys. We're home.

Upstairs in the bathroom. I lock the door.

Pause.

Nothing. Nothing comes. I look in the mirror and
nothing comes. I hear you call up the stairs, asking if
I want tea and nothing comes.

The WOMAN *moans and attempts to rise, but slumps
back down. The* MAN *clears his throat and lights
another cigarette.*

I checked on the girl. She was still asleep. I wander
back downstairs. I find myself by the coat cupboard.
I open it and shit myself. I thought it was your ghost,
but it's only your long white lollipop-ladies overcoat

hanging there. Your lollipop stick stands there as well –
'Stop!' illuminated briefly as I walk inside and close
the door. 'Stop!' Is it some kind of message from
beyond your brain I think to myself.

It's dark in here . . . darker than the dark outside.
Darker than the shadows. I'm next to one of your old
coats. Not a poorly coat. An old one, from before.

The MAN lifts his hands to his face and smells them.
He takes deep breaths.

I'm next to you again. The old you. The you I know.
That makes me laugh. I put my head under your coat
and breathe you in. All of you. All over. I can almost
feel you warm by my side. You're with me, you're
with me, you're with me, you're with me! I can smell
you. I can smell you. I remember! I remember when
our kid took you out . . . I got you ready. Helped
you to put your tights on . . . you kept trying to put
both legs in the same hole, we shouted at each other,
we fell on the floor and we laughed. We laughed
like we'd laughed before. Before the lump. Before
the dark. You put your arms around me and you
kissed me. You looked at me and saw me. The last
time, the very last time you were you and I was me.
I remember . . .

I cry . . . my eyes pour . . . but I make no sound. The
lump is in my throat again. The lump from the room.
The lump you gave me. The lump that I forced down
as we walked home. The lump I tried to save till we
got back. The lump I didn't want you to see.

Beat.

Your lollipop stick falls and hits me on the head. I'm
under your coat. I'm a twenty-six-year-old man crying
in the darkness and your lollipop stick has just hit me

on the head . . . It fuckin' hurt as well . . . Maybe it is
a message I think or maybe it's just a falling lollipop
stick. Everything's gone . . . you're just a lovely smell
on an old coat. No memories, memories have decayed,
decomposed in your head. Black, rotten, putrid sludge.
Time stopped. All life stopped in this house when
thoughts stopped. When your thoughts stopped feeding
the walls.

I look at you, but I don't see you anymore. If you
could talk what would you say? Mmmm? . . .

MAN/WOMAN (*simultaneously*). If you/I could talk
what would you/I say.

The MAN *turns away and lights a cigarette. He
wanders slowly towards the shadows, where he stands
smoking.*

WOMAN. I'd say I hate . . . this dress. Hate the colour.
It looks like sack. Trim on the collar. Peter Pan
collar . . . Gyave . . . Iyave . . . seven and counting.
Seven for the seven days. Yes. Seven and counting
seven. For senniven . . . finseev . . . sauurrvev . . .
fannar . . . fanssrarven. What days? What they called
days? When do they come? How do come? Howmen-
in . . . Come light and dark. Mmmm. Always light an
a dark. Every dressincome round light an a dark. Blue
one. Green one. Red one. Blue . . . Red. All with the
collar. Flowers. All flowers. Bright flowers and swan.
Nice flower an a white swan. They flower me with
flowers. Flowers that can't smell. Flowers that don't . . .
pick. Flowers that don't . . . flowners that don't . . .
stand in the . . . things. The bird . . . things . . . the
swan things . . . Floweres . . . Flowers I piss on.
Flowers I shit on. Flat flowers. Flowers that getting
wash and fade. I've got them in bunches. All over
me bunches. Every dark and light. Bunches. I know

them . . . I know they are them . . . I know they are all.
I cannnnn . . . know.

*She looks at the audience and smiles at no-one in
particular. She focuses on nothing. Her face is blank.
She looks at the bench, makes to sit on it. An anxious
look crosses her face. She is incapable of following
through the movement. She stands. She has already
forgotten what she was going to do. She sighs and
smiles.*

It's all of an all. All of all, of all of it. I am. I alwayam.
It. Iyam here. I be am. Me. Me am. Is where it is for
me. This . . . all it am. Is all it is. All it is all . . .

She closes her eyes and quickly says . . .

Dark and a light . . . dark an a light. An in all flowers.
(*Slower.*) Them flowers that don't feel like them.
Floweds that don't smell like them. The space of it.
All in me and a out of me, the space of it. Quietlyness
space of it. Inside . . . me . . . inside me the space of it.
Of it all . . .

Pause.

I see an not see. I hear and not hear. To think the think
of things and not do. Not feel their . . . vermmm . . .
feelness. Not . . . mmmoove wivth the feelingness of
it. Not feel.

She starts to become very agitated.

Making a mess . . . offff me. A mess of myself. Oh
is terrible. Terrible, terrible, terrible, terrible, terrible.
Stop it! Stop it! Now! Don't want it . . . don't wantdo
. . . Think of yourself . . . Think of the others. What
musthey think . . . Whaaaam . . . whahaamaduy . . .
whamidey . . . whamuusey

She moans little animal moans.

Thoughts. The thought of it, the thinking of it. I see them, the thoughts. I sit and see them all. I see the people round me. Me. My mess. The scurrying. The worry. The rush. The smiles. The concern. The loathing. The disgust. The bile. The heaving. The bile. The smell. The wetness. The bile. The warmth.

She raises her face to an imaginary sun.

(*Whispered.*) The warmth. The warmth. The warmth. The sun on my face. Washing me, across me, in me, through me. It's me! I'm here. I'm here again and it's me. I'm here again and the flowers! I'm here again and the smell! I'm here again and the all of it! The completeness of it. Of me. I'm here in the hereness of it and I am. Knowing one will come . . . It'll come and I'll catch it. Grab it. Don't know what it's going to be. Don't care. Anything. Anything that takes me . . .

This wrongness. On my back. The mess between my legs. Between my legs. Oh god. The mess. The smell. Wiped. Powdered. Plastic pants.

My baby.

He stands. Watching me. Silently. Silently me. He doesn't speak. Don't hear his voice. No soft voice. No comfort. He doesn't touch. Stands away. I can feel the space. The distance of him. The loss of him. Oh, the loss. The things felt. Everything inside of him. All away. In the blackness of it he is. In the farness that it is. Out . . . in a goneness.

I. Can't. Smell. His. Him.

I can't smell that which is him. His him, see. His him that is part of me. The him, that makes him, him. That I no longer have. That he no longer sees. Or looks to

see. Or expects to see. He doesn't know I'm here and
that I still am. Am the one, the person in the flowers,
the one he knows. I'm flowered, I'm flowered, my
baby, I'm flowered. Standing watching. Watching,
watching. Clearing his throat. All the time clearing
his throat. He never got rid of the knot. Big . . . rises
up . . . all the time rises up. Big grey wave thing. Not
skin. Not muscle. Energy. A bile. A lump . . . all the
time it is.

*She becomes agitated, pulling at her dress. She speaks
faster.*

I know how he got it. I was there. In the place. In a
that room. I felt it. Felt it there. I became part of him.
Into his body. Into him. A part of me in him. Me in
him. A bad part of me in him. It wanaaammin . . .
wusss in . . . It was in the room with us. In the room
with the smiling people. In the room. Inre thre room.
Inaeroom, neroomah. (*Whispering.*) The knot was
there, the knot was there, the knot was there and it
was mine. It was mine and I gave it to him. I gave it
to him, I gave it to my son, I gave it to my son, I gave
it to my baby. In a room full of strangers asking
strange questions. I gave my son a knot. I gave him
me. A piece of me. Of me. Of me. Of me.

Elizabeth the Queen. The Thatcher . . . Is not
Christmas? . . . Don't know, luv . . . Bull, car, man.
Could you repeat please? Bullmaaah . . . car, sorry . . .
Try again . . . Bbbbul, car . . . man. No? Backwards.
Reverse them please . . . No if's and annnns, no if
andnns but's. Where are you? What country are you
in? What day is it? Don't know . . . don't ask sstu
milly mally thingys. I look at the strangers, the young
people. My son's people.

Smiling smiles of smiles and smiles and smiles and
smiles and smiling smiles of smiling smiles. Malinga

malyle, maliyle, malyle, malyle, smiles. Standing there and standing there. Stands my Baby standing. Not smiling malinga malyle smiles. But standing. His face is stiff. His face is angry. His face is hard. A rock.

His face is wet.

His face is wet.

My baby's face is wet.

A fly is buzzing around the room. A fly is buzzing around the room.

My baby's face is wet. My life has gone and a fly buzzes about the room.

My brightness has gone and a fly buzzes about the room.

My motherness that mothered him gone . . . zzzzz . . .

My fingertips that touched his face have gone . . . zzzzz . . .

The way I looked my looks, that made me, me, have gone . . .

My me has gone.

All that is me has gone . . .

All that I was has gone in the buzzing of a buzz.

Pause.

Oh the sadness of it. Oh how sad, how sad, how sad, how sad it all is. The terrible, terrible sadness.

I just want me again for a momentness.

That that I was. That that I was to be. To smell my baby. To use my fingertips. To wipe the wetness of it from his face. For a momentness of time. Is all, that is all, that is all.

Pause.

The sun is warm on my face. I sit in the centre of the
room. It pours through the window in front of me.
Behind the smiling people. Smiling their smiles of
smiles and smiles and smiles and smiles. They have
no eyes. They are dark and the sun is bright. But they
smile. Strangers' smiles. They've ended it. My world.
My me. They've questioned my world and they've
ended it. My baby and my's world. The world we lived
in, brought into this room, is gone. Stripped clean.
Stripped by questions. Nothing remains standing. Not
even you my baby, my baby with the wet face.

The MAN *walks over to her, and tenderly helps her to
her feet and gently sits her down on the bench. He sits
down beside her.*

MAN. I was eight, the needle nurse came to school.
I was so scared I couldn't catch my breath . . .
screamed the place down. The door opened and you
were there with the other mums. I ran to you. You held
me. You dressed me. You said I could come home. You
bought me an ice lolly. I held your hand and ran to
keep up with you as we walked. Walked home through
the streets with the sun on our faces . . .

*The sound of the projector gets louder, until we are
left with just the sound of the loose end as it slaps
around the spool. The lights slowly fade.*

Blackout.

A Nick Hern Book

Notes on Falling Leaves first published in Great Britain
as a paperback original in 2004 by Nick Hern Books Limited,
14 Larden Road, London W3 7ST in association with
the Royal Court Theatre, London

Cover image: Penny Mills

Typeset by Country Setting, Kingsdown, Kent, CT14 8ES
Printed and bound in Great Britain by Athenaeum Press Ltd,
Gateshead, Tyne and Wear

A CIP catalogue record for this book is available from
the British Library

ISBN 1 85459 804 X